Harry's monkey

Written by Robina Beckles Willson

Illustrated by Diana Catchpole

Harry wanted a pet.

'I wish I had a monkey,' he said
to his mum.

'You can't have a monkey as a pet,'
said Mum. 'Now go to sleep.'

2

Harry went to sleep.
In his sleep he saw a monkey.
'You will make a good pet,'
said Harry. 'Come down and
play with me.'

But Monkey jumped on to the bed...

and then
on to a
chair...

and then he jumped all over the room.
'Stop, stop!' said Harry.

When Harry tried to catch him,
Monkey climbed up the curtain.
'You must come down,' said Harry.
'My mum will be cross with you.'

Monkey jumped on to a chair.

He put Harry's cap on his head and made a face in the mirror.

Harry laughed. Then he made
a face in the mirror too.

Then Monkey saw Harry's drum.
'BANG! BANG! BANG!' he went.
'Stop that!' called Harry. 'My mum
will be cross with you.'

'Let's go down the stairs and find
something for you to eat,' said Harry.
Monkey went down the stairs
very fast.

Harry gave Monkey a banana, but
Monkey wanted all the bananas.
He couldn't stop eating them.

'Stop!' said Harry. 'Look at all the
banana skins. My mum will be cross
if you eat all our bananas.'

'Come on,' said Harry. 'Let's go and play in our garden.'

But Monkey didn't want to play.
He wanted to jump up on the
washing line.
'Stop!' called Harry. 'You can't play
on the line.'

But Monkey liked going up and
down on the washing line.
'I must stop him,' said Harry.

Harry jumped up.
'Got you, Monkey!' he said.
But then Harry and Monkey and
the washing line all fell down.
'Oh no!' said Harry.

Just then Harry opened his eyes.

'I don't want to have a monkey

as a pet.'

Then Harry saw his toy monkey

and said, 'But I do want you.'